PRAYER THAT BRINGS RESULTS

Transforming Your Life Through Prayer

DANIEL W. PRINGLE, SR

Copyright © 2016 Daniel Pringle

ISBN:1519763808
ISBN-13:9781519763808

Prayer That Brings Results

ISBN:
ISBN-13:

CONTENTS

1

Facing the Impossible

The things which are impossible with men
are possible with God
-Luke 18:27

Life is not an easy journey, even when you become a believer. We all will face situations in our lives that will be completely out of our control and ability to manage. There will always be times when life comes at you and presents to you some critical crises that will demand that you must acknowledge that you need the hand of God to move on your behalf. You do not have to allow your situation to overwhelm you. We serve a God that loves us so much that during those difficult times, we can come to him in prayer and receive grace, peace, strength, and direction for what life throws at us.

**These things I have spoken to you, that in
Me you may have peace. In the world you
will have tribulation; but be of good cheer,
I have overcome the world.**
(John 16:33)

Yes, in this lifetime we will have tribulation. However, Christ has overcome the world, and through Him we can overcome as well.

I want to share with you some powerful principles that have given me strength to overcome the most difficult situations in my life through prayer. There was a time when I wasn't getting results in prayer. However, when the Holy Spirit began to teach me about the prayer of supplication, I began to see incredible results in my life.

Much that has been written about prayer. My intention is to give you tools to make your prayer more powerful, effective, to produce the desired results in your life. However, reading about prayer will not make your prayers more effective. Only when you implement the strategies I outline in this book will you begin to see results. I am going to walk you through in a simple way how to increase the results in prayer.

Our God is a God of the impossible. At a time when Abraham and Sarah were well beyond the age of bearing children the bible tells us in Genesis 18: 14 "Is anything too hard for the Lord?" If there were anything beyond the scope of God, then he would not be God. We know that there is nothing that God cannot do. There is no problem that you may be facing in which God does not have the power to overcome. Our God is a powerful God. However, because of the authority structure that God has established between heaven and earth, there are some things that will not be accomplished unless someone here on earth prays for it. God is looking for someone on the earth to give Him access through prayer to intervene in the affairs of man. All throughout the Bible, we see God doing things on behalf of His people that with man would be impossible. God is about to turn your impossible into a possibility. As Jesus said in Luke 18:27, "the things which are impossible with men are possible with God."

If you are faced with a seemingly impossible situation—whether it be physical, emotional, financial, or a relational—I have good news for you: With God, *all things* are possible. Not some things, not a few things, but all things are possible. Don't give up, don't lose heart, and don't lose hope. Our God is a specialist in turning impossible situations around. He is ready and willing to get involved on your behalf. As a matter of fact, He is waiting for you to invite him into your situation so that He can show Himself strong.

There are some things that will not be done unless we pray. You cannot afford to leave things to chance. You cannot sit back passively to see how things will turn out. You cannot leave your destiny hanging in the balance of circumstances or people. You must take the initiative through prayer to get God involved.

One of the primary characteristics of the newly born church was prayer. Prayer was an integral part of their lives. Prayer was an active part of them exercising their faith. In the book of Acts 2:42 we read that the church "continued steadfastly in the apostles' doctrine and fellowship, in breaking of bread, and in prayers."

The early church demonstrated power as a result their dedication to prayer. Peter and John had just been arrested after a lame man had been healed by a gate called beautiful. While in custody Peter and John began to speak with boldness under the inspiration of the Holy Spirit as they were addressing the Sanhedrin. When the Sanhedrin saw the boldness of Peter and John they knew they were uneducated and untrained men, but they marveled, and realized they had been with Jesus.

The Sanhedrin could not refute the miraculous healing that took place, so they conferred among themselves to figure out what to do with them. In order that this would not spread, the Sanhedrin threatened and commanded them not to speak or teach in the name of Jesus again. The threats did not stop the apostles, Peter said, "whether it is right in the sight of God to listen to you more than to God, you judge. For we cannot but speak the things we have seen and heard" (Acts 4:19-29).

Once Peter and John were released they each went to their own company and began to report everything that had happened. This was a great victory for the church. Now instead of backing up off the threats, they began to pray for God to release more miracles and boldness. After they had prayed, the place began to shake, and power was released.

And when they had prayed, the place where they were assembled together was shaken; and they were all filled with the Holy Spirit, and they spake the word of God with boldness. (Acts 4:31)

Can you see why satan does not want the churches to come together and pray? He is afraid of the shaking that is going to take place. Power is multiplied when God's people come together to pray. God give us Holy Ghost shakings again!

In Acts 12 the apostle James had just been killed by Herod, and now Peter was awaiting his execution. His execution was being delayed because it was the Passover and Herod needed to wait until it was over so as not to stir up trouble. However, during this delay constant prayer was made for him by the church. Verse 5 states; "Peter was therefore kept in prison: but constant prayer was offered to God for him by the church." They didn't conduct a board meeting to try to come up with ways to raise money to get him out of prison, they prayed.

Our churches need to get back to the foundation of prayer. When they prayed, angelic forces were activated. On the night that Herod was to bring Peter out to be executed an angel appeared in his prison cell. Peter was under heavy guard by Herod, but that did not hinder his deliverance.

When the angel appeared, he awoke Peter out of his sleep, immediately the chains that were restraining him were broken off. Once the angel led him out of the city he went to the very house where they were praying. When he knocked on the door, a girl name Rhoda opened the door for him. She was so overwhelmed by his appearance that she closed the door to tell the others that the one who they were praying for was at the door. When they finally let him in, they were all astonished by his appearance.

Something supernatural takes place when Gods people begin to pray. Prayer activates the supernatural to take place in your life. God wants to do things in your life that is going to astonish you.]

I have faced many situations in my life in which I could not change the circumstances had it not been for prayer. I was once faced with an impossible financial situation that I could not fix. I simply did not have the resources in the bank, nor did I have anyone that I could borrow a large sum of money from. Nevertheless, the Holy Spirit spoke to my heart while I was in prayer and said, *"Let me teach you how to pray the money into your life."* So, I signed up in the School of the Holy Spirit. The subject was the prayer of supplication. The classroom was my closet. My professor was the Holy Spirit.

God began to take everything that I thought I knew about prayer, erased it, and started the foundations of approaching Him, understanding my identity, getting His attention, and teaching me about the prayer of supplication and how to prepare it. I have now adopted this method and have experienced a dramatic increase in answered prayer.

I am not saying that this is a formula that is going to bring results in all your prayers. However, I strongly believe that the principles outlined in this book will no doubt increase them being answered, and you will begin on a new journey in prayer. I've learned that if I received more results by spending quality strategic time in prayer, I would be doing a lot more praying rather than trying to figure things out on my own.

One of the most critical prayers that a believer will pray is called the prayer of supplication. The prayer of supplication is a type of prayer that signifies a request for benefits. These benefits may include concerns about any area of your life including purpose, desire, needs, and problems. The prayer of supplication must be prayed in faith. This prayer is based on a promise of God, found in His Word. The manifestation of your prayer is received by faith. That faith is generated by hearing the Word of God.

The word *"supplication"* means to request or to petition. In other words, you are coming to God requesting something of Him. God has provided for us a type of prayer because we are in need. The prayer of supplication is a tremendous tool that we can utilize to have our needs met. When we approach God in this manner we will see the demonstration of a father's love for his children.

If you then, being evil, know how to give good gifts to your children, how much

**more will your Father who is in heaven
give good things to those who ask Him.
(Matthew 7:11)**

Every parent will do everything within their
power to help their children when they are in need. I
remember my parents telling me when I was a child,
"You'll have to wait till I get paid again; we just don't
have the money right now." It's not that they didn't
want to get me what I needed, but they had limited
resources. But we serve a God that is not only willing
to bless us, but He has all the resources at His
disposal.

The prayer of supplication is not something new.
We see several occurrences in the Bible of people
using this type prayer. Hannah used this prayer
while she could not give her husband children.

Elkanah had another wife, Peninnah, who had no
problem giving Elkanah children. However,
Peninnah continually provoked Hannah because she
could not have children. There are some people that
seem like their assignment in their life is to make you
miserable. Hannah had gone to the temple to pray
and said, O Lord of hosts, if You will indeed look on
the affliction of Your maidservant and remember me,
and not forget Your maidservant, but will give Your
maidservant a male child, then I will give him to the
Lord all the days of his life, and no razor shall come
upon his head. (1 Samuel 1:11)

We see that Hannah asked for a specific
request. She wanted not just child, but a male child.

Hannah desired to have a son yet her womb was shut up. The Lord shut up her womb. It wasn't satan, it was the Lord. God had prevented her from having children at that time. I believe that the reason that God did so is that He was giving Eli, who was the high priest now, an opportunity to repent and get his house in order. God wanted to time the birth of Samuel to release him at the right time to intersect with the life of Eli. Sometimes, the scope of our prayers go beyond us. There are other people that our prayers are connected to that we may not realize. It may appear that your prayer is being delayed— that doesn't mean it is being denied. It just may be postponed because God is aligning His answers to you with the lives of other people. Paul encourages us with this; "And let us not grow weary while doing good, for in due season we shall reap if we do not lose heart" (Gal. 6:9).

Eli had accused Hannah of being drunk because he saw her lips moving but didn't hear her. However, Hannah had replied and told Eli; "No, my lord, I am a woman of sorrowful spirit. I have drunk neither wine nor intoxicating drink, but have poured out my soul before the Lord. Do not consider your maid servant a wicked woman, for out of the abundance of my complaint and grief I have spoken until now" (1 Sam.1:15-16).

In other words, she was in such desperate need that out of the abundance of her pain, she poured out her heart to God. By faith, she said to God, "Remember me!" She understood the principle that

God is a rewarder of those that diligently seek him. You may be in a situation and saying God, "I am in need and in a desperate situation, remember me!"

Eli answered her, "Go in peace, and the God of Israel grant your petition that you have asked of him" (1 Sam. 1:17). Now you can sense that Hannah's confidence rising as she then asks, "Let your maidservant find favor in your sight, so the woman went her way and ate, and her face was no longer sad" (1 Sam.1:18). After Eli gave the blessing of God granting her petition, Hannah now asks for favor as well. Because of her prayer of supplication, she gave birth to Samuel. She had asked for a son. Samuel was her request. He was the manifestation of her petition. However, after Samuel was born, she gave birth to five more children! The five other children were the favor that was granted. Not only did God grant her the petition, but also gave her favor. When you can come to the place where God grants your petition, and you birth your Samuel, that is just the beginning, the favor that is going to be released upon your life is going to open the door for more! This is Hannah's response, "For this child I prayed, and the Lord has granted me my petition which I asked of Him" (1 Sam.1:27).

It was through the prayer of supplication that Hannah received her Samuel. What is it that you need God to open for you in the same way Hannah's womb opened? Hannah did not go to her husband to fix her problem—she took it to God. Everyone has their own way of handling a difficult situation.

Unfortunately, for many of us, the last resort is going to God in prayer. If we were go to Him in prayer first, we would save ourselves all the emotional energy that we would have expended worrying about how things are going to work out.

God has given us the prayer of supplication to use in our lives for whatever we need. Yet, many people don't know how to utilize this powerful prayer to bring about miraculous results. If you are ready to see results in your life of prayer, then let's get ready to delve into the secrets that are hidden through the Word of God and uncover knowledge and wisdom to transform your life.

2

The Power of Prayer

*The effective, fervent prayer of a
righteous man avails much.*
- James 5:16

I have been a person of prayer for as long as I can remember. When I first became a believer, it was easier for me to pray than to understand the Word of God. The church that I was attending had prayer on Tuesday nights, but nobody taught me *how* to pray. I would find my favorite spot and kneel. We would cry out to God, and we spent a lot of time thanking and praising God. Basically, I felt more like I as preaching to God while I was on my knees rather than coming to Him in prayer and supplication. As I began to struggle in areas such as my career, finances, and family, I needed direction. I began to spend a lot more time in prayer, but I didn't see many results. It left me feeling disappointed and abandoned. I would hear about other people getting their prayers answered, but I felt ignored. I began to fear that I was wasting my time.

Even though I felt that I was not getting results in my prayer life this didn't stop me from praying. I decided to take the initiative and immerse myself to learn all I can about prayer. I read countless books on prayer. I went through the bible to see what it says about prayer, as well as talked with people who were well seasoned in prayer. As my understanding began to increase, my prayer life began to develop and mature.

Prayer was not just a religious exercise I went through; it became a vibrant part of my spiritual development. Yes, there were many struggles along the way. Letting go of unfruitful habits and learning new productive methods of prayer took time and discipline. One of first things that began to shift was my motive for prayer. I soon began to realize that prayer was not just a means of getting God to do something for me, but rather it was a means of enjoying Him. We were made to enjoy His presence. This was a new attitude that I had to develop. Now when I come to God in prayer I am coming to him to enjoy His presence. To be in God's presence seemed to make all the issues of my life diminish. Once my attitude and approach towards God changed so did my prayers. I made enjoying God my priority in prayer, then because He cares for the things that are pressing in life, I can also a present my needs to Him. Not only was I getting to know Him more intimately, but I also began to experience answers to prayer.

It wasn't until I implemented the principles of prayer that I learned, that I began to see results in my life. As the scripture declares, "My people are destroyed for a lack of knowledge" (Hos. 4:6). If we are not getting our prayers answered, then I don't think that it is because of something on God's end but rather we are lacking knowledge in how prayer operates. Prayer is God's concept, and if God is the one who came up with the concept of prayer, then I would welcome the opportunity for Him to teach me.

To get powerful results in prayer, we must establish the foundations of prayer. We cannot have the fruit of answered prayer unless we have a proper root system. That root system is founded in understanding our authority in prayer. Without a proper understanding of spiritual authority in prayer, you will never be able to stand in a place of confidence and expectation. To gain understanding of our spiritual authority, we must look at the beginning of the relationship between God and man.

SPIRITUAL AUTHORITY

Prayer is a result of God's established authority structure between heaven and earth. When God created man, He gave man dominion. God now gave man authority to govern in the earth. God said in Genesis 1:26-27; Let us make man in Our image, according to Our likeness; let them have dominion over the fish of the sea, over the birds of the air, and over the cattle, over all the earth and over every creeping thing that creeps on the earth.

The earth is still the Lords, but He has now given man the legal authority to steward the earth. Adam is now God's representative in the earth. Adam was now the authorized to manage the affairs on the

14

earth. The authority to steward the earth had now been conferred upon Adam. David says, "The heaven, even the heavens, are the Lord's; But the earth He has given to the children of men" (Ps. 115:16). The Hebrew word for *"given"* means *"assigned."* The earth is now Adam's assignment. Adam is now the legal representative on the earth for God, and his assignment was this planet. However, when Adam sinned against God, by disobeying, and eating the fruit of the tree of knowledge of good and evil, he now submitted himself to satan and therefore relinquished the authority God invested in him. Thus, satan now has authority in the earth realm. Satan is now called "the god of this age" (2 Cor. 4:4), as well as "the prince and power of the air" (Eph. 2:2). Therefore, Jesus had to come in the form of a man, because God had initially released the authority to humanity, specifically Adam. Therefore, to get that authority back, Jesus had to come as the last Adam to deliver man from the power of satan and take back the authority that Adam forfeited.

After Jesus was baptized by John he was immediately led by the Spirt into the wilderness to be tempted of the devil. Satan now had authority in the earth. Look at what the gospel of Luke records;

Then the devil, taking Him up on a high mountain, showed Him all the kingdoms of the world in a moment of time. And the devil said to Him, " All this authority I will give You, and their glory, for this has been

delivered to me, and I give it to whomever I wish. (Luke 4:5-6)

Notice that Jesus did not refute the fact that satan had the authority over the kingdoms, because it had been handed over to him by Adam. Satan was willing to give the authority of the kingdoms to Jesus, if He would fall down and worship him. Whoever you submit to has authority over your life. Let me put it another way, whatever you worship has control over your heart. Thank God that Jesus refused the offer!

It was through the perfect obedience of Christ to the will of God and the completed work on Calvary that Jesus Christ could regain the authority that Adam forfeited. This is what Christ accomplished through Calvary. He lived a sinless, obedient life, which now qualified Him to take back the authority Adam lost. After the resurrection, Jesus states "All authority has been given to Me in heaven and on earth" (Matt. 28:18).

Because of the resurrection and ascension of Jesus, the same power that raised Christ from the dead is now working in you. The same power that God exerted in Christ when He raised him from the dead is in us. We are now the body of Christ here on the earth. God has placed the keys of authority in the hands of His church. Jesus states in Matthew 16:19, "I will give you the keys of the kingdom of heaven, and whatever you bind on earth will be bound in heaven, and whatever you loose on earth will be loosed in heaven".

What does spiritual authority have to do with prayer? We are now His body in the earth, and when we pray in His name, we are now praying as if He is praying through us. The same authority that Jesus operated in while He was on the earth is available for us to pray today. Also, when we pray, we are functioning as priests here on the earth. It is our privilege and priestly responsibility to come to God and pray His kingdom into the earth.

HEAVENS INVOLVEMENT

Because of the finished work of Christ, the authority to govern the earth has now been placed back into the hands of the redeemed. Now when we pray, we are inviting God to intervene in the affairs here on the earth. Nothing will happen in the earth realm without the active or passive permission of man, who is its legal authority. If we don't pray there are some things that will not be accomplished in the earth. Prayer is man giving God the legal right and permission to interfere in earth's affairs. Even Jesus instructed the disciples to pray, "...Your kingdom come. Your will be done on earth as it is in heaven" (Matthew 6:10). Prayer is vital for the will of God being accomplished in the earth. Prayer is now the primary way to get heaven involved in the earthly arena.

If my people, who are called by my name, will humble themselves, and pray and seek My face, and turn from their wicked ways,

then I will hear from heaven, and will forgive their sin, and heal their land.
(2 Chronicles 7:14)

So, heaven is waiting for someone to give access in earth to intervene. Prayer is not an option, but a necessity!

So I sought for a man among them who would make a wall, and stand in the gap before Me on behalf of the land, that I should not destroy it; but I found no one. Therefore I have poured out My indignation on them. I have consumed them with the fire of My wrath.
(Ezekiel 22:30)

God said He was looking for a man, a person who would stand in the gap before Him and intercede, yet no one was available. Because no one was available He poured out His wrath. Had there been an intercessor present, then their prayer would have prevented God from pouring out His wrath. I wonder what things could have been prevented had we been more sensitive to the Spirit of God when He was leading us to pray. Yet because we were so caught up in our own lives that events took place that didn't have to happen had we prayed. God is looking for people who will stand in the gap!

PUTTING POWER TO WORK

One of the greatest deceptions of the enemy is to make you think that you have no authority and power. As a born-again believer, you have the power to alter circumstances, change outcomes, and remove hindrances. This is why the Apostle Paul prayed that prayer to the church in Ephesus.

> **...and what is the exceeding greatness of His power toward us who believe, according to the working of His mighty power which He worked in Christ when He raised Him from the dead and seated Him at His right hand in heavenly places far above all principality and might and dominion, and every name that is named not only in this age but also in that which is to come. And He put all things under His feet, and gave Him to be the head over all things to the church, which is His body, the fullness of Him who fills all in all.**
> **(Ephesians 1:19-23)**

Paul wanted us to understand the authority that you and I now possess as believers. The same power and authority that raised Christ from the dead and seated Him at the right hand in heavenly places is now inside of us. He is far above any other power. God has now put all things under the authority of Christ. Now the church is the body of Christ and our inheritance is the power that was given to Christ by God is available for us NOW. It is time to exercise that authority through prayer. When we pray, we are now releasing that authority and power that Christ obtained. I especially like what the Amplified Version says:

And [so that you can know and understand] what is the immeasurable and unlimited and surpassing greatness of His power in and for us who believe, as demonstrated in the working of His mighty strength.

That immeasurable, unlimited, and surpassing power is working in us and is working for us. Now we need to put the power to work. That power is released in our lives when we come to God in prayer. We are not sending up empty-handed prayers to God. Our prayers are packed with the power and authority of Christ himself.

PRAYER THAT APPLIES FORCE
The effective, fervent prayer of a righteous man avails much. Elijah was a man with a nature like ours, and he prayed earnestly that it would not rain; and it did not rain on the land for three years and six months. And he prayed again, and the heaven gain rain, and the earth produces its fruits.

(James 5:16-18)

The phrase *"effectually fervent"* is from the Greek word *energeo,* that means *"active and efficient."* Your prayer is active, it is at work, and it is going into the heavens and shifting things. Prayer is releasing kingdom power into the earth realm. You are releasing power that is designed to produce powerful results. The word *"avails"* means, *"exercises and applies great force."* When you pray correctly, you are applying great force. You are putting pressure on spiritual powers that are limiting you, causing them to release their hold. The active and efficient prayer of a righteous man exercises and applies great force.

Elijah had the same nature as ours. He was just as human as you and I. He had issues just like anyone else. However, when he presented himself to Ahab uninvited, unannounced and declared that it would not rain or dew except according to his word, the heavens shut down for the next 3 years and six months. Where did Elijah get this faith? We know that faith comes by hearing and hearing by the Word of God (Rom. 10:17). You will find that the faith that supported the prayer of Elijah was found in Deuteronomy 28 where God tells the people that if they go after other gods that the heavens which were over their heads would turn to brass, and the earth would turn to iron, and the rain would be turned to powder (vs 23).

Elijah was fully acquainted with the Word of God. He knew that if God's people would go after other gods then he was now the authorized agent to command the heavens to turn to brass, the earth to iron, and the rain to powder. His confidence and prayer was not based on his own word, but rather on what God had already said. And when he prayed that it would not rain, yet the heavens responded by closing for the next three years and six months.

Then, God told him to go hide by a brook called Cherith. Why would God tell Elijah to hide himself after he had just presented himself to Ahab in boldness and confidence? The reason being is that Elijah declared that it would not rain except according to his word, and had King Ahab killed Elijah out of anger and furry, the drought would still be in effect today. God had to hide Elijah to protect him from Ahab, so when the time came to pray again he was preserved to speak to the heavens and release the rain.

Once the children of God had turned their hearts back to the Lord, Elijah prayed again, and the heavens responded by releasing the rain. When the heavens responded by opening and releasing rain, the earth could bring forth fruit.

When there is no rain, there is no harvest. Without the rain, the economy had gone into recession. When the rain was released, the economy was revived. That demonstrates the power that is available to us!

When our prayers are grounded in the Word of God, then they become active and efficient, applying great force that is released into the heavens that will produce powerful results in our lives.

3

The Fruit of Answered Prayer

Whatever you ask in My name, that I will do, that the Father may be glorified in the Son. If you ask anything in My name, I will do it.

-John 14:13-14

God wants you to experience the fruit of answered prayer. God takes pleasure in answering our prayers. He is the One that designed prayer, and prayer is meant to be answered. If you don't have this one issue settled, you will never come to Him with an expectation. Prayer is not designed just to relieve you of your distress. It is designed to be answered when you understand how prayer works. There are several promises in God's Word to prayer being answered. As a matter of fact, as soon as we ask, God answers. But sometimes those answers are revealed in His timing, not ours.

He shall call upon Me, and I will answer him; I will be with him in trouble; I will deliver him and honor him. (Psalm 91:15)

I know that this sounds simple. Unless you are absolutely convinced in your heart that it is God's will to answer your prayer, then you will not pray at all. You will just leave things to chance. Prayer is designed by God. He is the one who came up with the concept. Since it is designed by God, then it should work for you. If God is the one who came up with the concept, don't you think that prayer is meant to be answered?

I used to spend hours in prayer, and often repeating myself, praying extremely loud so everyone in the whole neighborhood could hear me. My times of prayer were intense. I came out feeling pumped up if you know what I mean. I realized that God is not hard of hearing. I don't have to pray loud to get Him to listen. I think that I prayed loud because maybe somewhere deep down inside I was trying to convince God to hear me. If I have a need, if I am in a desperate situation and I am in distress, then I need to know that God is listening. I needed God not just to hear me—I needed some answers. I don't just want to pray to God just as a form of spiritual therapy session. What good would that do in my life? It might make me feel better, but what about the results?

I am not saying that there is anything wrong with praying loud. There are still times I pray loud, but my motive is not because I am trying to get God's attention, but because of there is a release of emotions because of the affliction that I may be going through. When you pray, your spirit as well as your soul gets involved. If you are in distress, you can release it when you pray. There's nothing wrong with that. Listen, if you can't release how you feel to God, who can you release it to? Even David made this a practice in his life when he encourages us "pour out your heart before Him" (Ps. 62:8).

There are times when we come to God in prayer and we just need to know that God is hearing us and we are not wasting our time. This is such a deception of the enemy, that when you are praying, satan is trying to whisper in your ear that God is not hearing you.

THE PRIORITY OF PRAYER

Prayer seems to be at the bottom of most believers' priorities. Many people say that they simply don't have the time to pray. Our lives are filled with obligations, appointments and various other demands. By the time the day is over most people are too exhausted from the demands of the day that they simply don't have the energy to pray. Each day has its own set of challenges. There are some that are expected and some that show up unexpected. I wonder how much of our time is consumed by trying to solve problems in our lives? What if we believed in the power of prayer to the degree that we spent more time in prayer than trying to solve our problems? I believe that if we saw an increase in the results of answered prayer, we would be doing a lot more praying.

Jesus earthly ministry was remarkably brief, barely three years long. Yet in those three years, He spent a great amount of time in prayer. The gospels record that Jesus habitually rose early in the morning, often before daybreak to commune with His father. In the evening, He would frequently go to the Mount of Olives or some other quiet spot to pray, usually alone. Prayer was the spiritual air that Jesus breathed every day of His life. He practiced an unending communion between Himself and the Father. Since the ultimate purpose of our salvation is to glorify God and to bring us into intimate, rich fellowship with Him, failure to seek God in prayer is to deny that purpose. "What we have seen and heard we proclaim to you also," says the Apostle John, "that you also may have fellowship with us; and indeed our fellowship is with the Father, and His Son Jesus Christ" (1 Jn. 1:3).

David was a man of prayer as well. He made it a custom to seek God early in the morning. In Psalm 5:3 he says; "My voice You shall hear in the morning, O LORD; In the morning, I will direct it to You, And I will look up."

Each day presents its own set of challenges and difficulties. There will be interactions with people, some may be pleasant, while others may be not so pleasant. Each day you will face issues that will require choices, decisions, and even involve your emotions. One of the primary benefits of making prayer a priority in the morning is that even before the challenges of the day have an opportunity to interfere with your peace, you can set the tone of your day through prayer. You are taking the initiative. You are being proactive rather than reacting to the course of the day's events. Jesus told the disciples to pray, "Your kingdom come. Your will be done on earth, as it is in heaven" (Matt. 6:10). The kingdom of God is the rule of God. You are inviting God's kingdom to rule in every sphere of your life. The kingdom of God is living a life of righteousness, peace and joy in the Holy Spirit (Romans 14:17). Take the time to involve the Kingdom of God by making declarations of righteousness, peace, and joy over your family, your marriage, children, and occupation. Release God's peace even before problems arise. Release His joy before attitudes from others have an opportunity to be displayed. Take control of your day by releasing the atmosphere of God's kingdom in the morning.

THE FRUIT OF PEACE

Be anxious for nothing, but in everything by prayer and supplication, with thanksgiving, let your requests be made known unto God: and the peace of God, which surpasses all understanding, will guard your hearts and minds through Christ Jesus. (Philippians 4:6-8)

One of the greatest benefits to prayer is

experiencing God's peace. The apostle Paul instructs us not to be anxious and worry, instead pray about everything. When we pray rather than worry we will experience God's supernatural peace.

Worry is evidence that we lack trust. When we worry, we are not moving in faith. When we are not in faith, we cannot please God. The root of worry is fear. Often fear of the unknown, fear of tomorrow.

Anxiety is a reaction to stresses like financial challenges, health problems, and relationship issues. We all experience some form of stress in our lives. Reacting to stress in the wrong way will produce worry, or anxiety. Worry is a powerful state of mind that depletes you of peace, joy, and strength. Excessive worrying will cause your mind and body will go into overdrive as you constantly focus on what might happen. Chronic worrying affects you daily life so much that it can interfere with your appetite, and lifestyle habits, your relationships, and sleep patterns and job performance.

Worry begins when you take just one thought that is contrary to God's provision. You cannot afford to take even one negative thought. One negative thought is a seed that you don't need the harvest of in your life right now. Do not accept one thought that negates God's promises.

You may feel as though you have no control over the stressful situation. The good news is that when you offer to God your prayer of supplication He promises that "the peace of God, which surpasses all understanding, will guard your hearts and minds in

Christ Jesus" (Phil. 4:7).

There is an inner calm or tranquility that is promised to every believer who has a thankful attitude based on what unwavering confidence that God is able and willing to do what is best for His children. This peace surpasses all comprehension. It transcends human intellect. God promised that "You will keep him in perfect peace, Whose mind is stayed on You, Because he trusts in You" (Is. 26:3).

Paul tells us that this peace will *"guard"* your hearts and minds. This was a military term meaning *"to keep watch over."* God's peace guard's believers from anxiety, doubt, fear and distress. God guards your whole inner being with His peace.

Therefore I say to you, do not worry about your life, what you will eat or what you will drink; nor about your body, what you will put on. Is not life more than food and the body more than clothing? Look at the birds of the air, for they neither sow nor reap nor gather into barns, yet your heavenly Father feeds them. Are you not of more value than they? (Matthew 6:25-26)

If by God's providential care, He takes complete responsibility and care for birds and flowers, how much more will God providentially care for those that are made in His image and carry His spirit?

I've never seen a worried bird. Worry is seated in our lack of understanding of our value to God.

Whatever God creates, He provides for. If God sustains and provides for birds, which are not even made in his image and likeness, how much more will God provide for us? We need to see that the reason God wants to answer our prayer is that we are valuable to Him. You are valuable to God. Your problems are important to Him. If you are experiencing worry, then you need to renew your mind on how valuable you are to God. Your value is not based on your performance but on His love.

Jesus didn't say, "cut down your worrying." He states "don't worry." The King James Version says, "take no thought." When your mind tries to take a negative thought and you begin to meditate on that thought it turns to worry. At that moment, you need to intercept that thought and change your focus. To experience God's peace, you must change your focus from what is trying to cause you to worry and allow those concerns to be shaped into prayers. Don't focus on the stressful situation, but rather place your focus on kingdom realities and God's provision for your situation. Get out of worry, and get in faith through adoration, thanksgiving, and meditating on God's word. When you do, this worry will no longer dominate your thought life. Let the sound of your prayer be faith filled words. Heaven is waiting to intervene. It's time to exercise your God given privileges in prayer.

GOD IS GLORIFIED

In the disciples' hour of loss at the departure of

Jesus, He comforts them with the means that would provide them with the necessary resources to accomplish their task without His immediate presence, which they had come to depend on. Jesus states;

> **Whatever you ask in My name, that I will do, that the Father may be glorified in the Son. If you ask anything in My name, I will do it. (John 14:13-14)**

To ask in Jesus's "name" does not mean to tack such an expression on the end of a prayer as a mere formula. It means that the prayer in Christ's name must be consistent with Christ's character. When you are praying in His name, it means you praying in His authority. You are using His authority. You are authorized to perform kingdom business because of His authority.

What caught my attention was when I read that He *"is glorified when I ask."* In other words, when we pray, and God answers our prayer, then it brings glory to Him. He is glorified when He answers our prayer. Christ is the head and Lord over the church. Therefore, if God does not answer our prayer, it doesn't' bring God glory. God is not glorified when you don't have your needs met. God is not glorified when you don't have the resources you need. Therefore, every opportunity for God to answer your prayer is an opportunity for Him to be glorified. When I understood this, my thinking shifted concerning prayer.

If you abide in Me, and My words abide in you, you will ask what you desire, and it shall be done for you. By this is My Father is glorified, that you bear much fruit; so you will be My disciples. (John 15:7)

The passage is primarily talking about Him being the vine and we abiding in Him. The result of our abiding in Him is that we can ask what we desire and it shall be done for us. Again, we see that God is glorified when we bear much fruit. The context indicates that we are asking God for something. The fruit that He is talking about is the fruit of what you have asked for being answered. God wants you to experience the fruit of answered prayer.

I want to show you the progression. It starts with abiding, then asking, then answering. Your answer is a result of your asking. Your asking is predicated on you abiding. So, it all begins with abiding, then asking, to finally answering. To *"abide in"* means to continue to live in. In other words, your life is so connected with God that your asking is a result of your abiding. It is His Spirit that is now prompting you to ask for what He already wants to give you. Your purpose and His purpose are so knit that the very thing that you are asking is what He impressed in you because of you abiding.

The word *"ask"* in this context means *"to make a claim of something due"*. You are not just saying, "Will you do this for me?" Rather you are placing a claim or demand on the power of God and His Word. You are not demanding God does it. You are placing a demand on the power available.

JOY IS FULL

And in that day, you will ask Me nothing. Most assuredly, I say to you, whatever you ask the Father in My name He will give you. Until now you have asked nothing My name. Ask, and you will receive, that your joy may be full. (John 16:23)

Here we see again another reason why God wants to answer your prayer. The reason is that your joy will be full. I had never thought about that. When God answers prayer, your joy is full. There is a joy that you experience every time that you see the hand of God moving in your behalf doing for you what you could not do for yourself. There is no joy when you are behind on your bills. There is no joy in experiencing defeat or failure. When God gives you the victory through prayer you will experience the joy of answered prayer.

HINDRANCES TO ANSWERED PRAYER

If our prayer is not being answered, then we need to examine as to whether there may be any hindrances on our part that we need to address. We must take inventory of our lives and adjust those things that are blocking our flow in prayer.

Prayer That Brings Results

<u>Iniquity</u>

The first area of course is sin, which separates us from God. Is there any secret or unconfessed sin that may be in our lives that we have not addressed? In Isaiah 59:1-2 he says;

Behold, the Lord's hand is not shortened, that it cannot save; Nor His ear heaven, that it cannot hear. But your iniquities have separated you from your God; and your sins have hidden His face from you, So that He will not hear.

It doesn't say that God is unable to do what you need done. The problem is that sin has separated us from God. Psalm 66:18-20 David states;

If I regard iniquity in my heart, the Lord will not hear. But certainly God has heard me; He has attended to the voice of my prayer. Blessed be God, Who has not turned away my prayer, Nor His mercy from me!

God has made provision for our sin through the sacrifice of Jesus Christ. If you have unconfessed sin in your life, take the time and humble yourself and confess your sin.

My little children, these things I write to you, so that you may not sin. And if anyone sins,

34

we have an Advocate with the Father, Jesus Christ the righteous. (1 John 2:1)

The term *"advocate"* means *"helper"*, one who comes alongside. A modern concept of the term would be a defense attorney. Although satan prosecutes believers before God due to their sin, Jesus Christ's high priestly ministry guarantees our acquittal.

Doubt

The second hindrance to answered prayer is doubt. This is one area many people struggle with. James 1:6-7 instructs us;

But let him ask in faith, with no doubting, for he who doubts is like a wave of the sea driven and tossed by the wind. For let not that man suppose that he will receive anything from the Lord; he is a double-minded and, unstable in all his ways.

Prayer must be offered with a confident trust in a sovereign God without any doubt. Doubting refers to having one's thinking divided within himself, not merely because of mental indecision but of an inner moral conflict or distrust in God. This is where many people lose the battle of having their prayers answered. To counteract this, you must continue to feed your faith on the promises of God.

Wrong Motives

It is not enough to ask for good thing, we must ask with proper intention. Improper cravings and misplaced desires will not be answered in prayer. In James 4:3 the apostle writers to his readers, "You ask and do not receive, because you ask amiss, that you may spend it on your pleasures."

You will hinder your prayer when you are motivated by personal gratification and selfish desire. Unbelievers seek things for their own pleasure, not the honor and glory of God

KEYS TO ANSWERED PRAYER

Prayer is more than a formula but a posture of the heart. These are keys that we must continue to develop in our lives if we want to see our prayers answered.

Humility

Humility is a prerequisite to getting your prayers answered. Humility is the posture of the heart that expresses absolute dependence on God. Pride is the sin that will cause great calamity and God is opposed to the proud.

If my people who are called by my name will humble themselves, and pray and seek My face, and turn from their wicked ways, then I will hear from heaven, and will forgive their sin and heal their land.

(2 Chronicles. 7:14)

Some people think that they are self- sufficient, independent of God. This is what happened to satan, he became proud and lifted up and tried to exalt himself above God. This is that attitude that believers are to demonstrate. Humility is not natural for the unregenerate. It was the attribute of humility that Christ demonstrated when He became a man.

Let this mind (attitude) be in you which was also in Christ Jesus, who, being in the form of God, did not consider it robbery to be equal with God, but made Himself of no reputation, taking the form of a bondservant, and coming in the likeness of men. And being found in appearance as a man, He humbled Himself and became obedient to the point of death, even the death of the cross. (Philippians 2:5-8)

Faith

Faith is what pleases God. Faith possesses a sound that gets God's attention. Without faith you cannot please God. Anything that is not done in faith is sin (Rom.14:23). Simple faith is taking God at his Word. When you have a Word from God, you have faith.

But without faith it is impossible to please Him, for he that comes to God must believe that He is, and that He is a rewarder of those who diligently seek Him. (Hebrews 11:6)

When it comes to prayer, faith is mandatory. God does not respond to our crisis as much as He responds to our faith. Let your prayers be filled with faith.

<u>Obedience</u>

When it comes to prayer being answered, obedience is critical. John says that whatever we ask we are going to receive because we are obeying the Word of God.

And whatever we ask, we receive of Him, because we keep his commandments, and do those things that are pleasing in His sight.

(1 John 3: 22)

When you obey the Word of God then you are living in a way that is pleasing to God. When your ways please God, your steps are ordered of the Lord. You cannot pick and choose what you are going to obey and not obey. Make walking in obedience a daily habit.

John then goes on to say "And this is His commandment: That we should believe on the name of His Son Jesus Christ, and love one another, as He gave us commandment." (1 Jn. 3:23). Faith and love are the primary laws that we are to walk in. If you walk in faith and walk in love towards other people in a consistent manner even when you don't feel like it, you will not have any problems getting powerful results in prayer.

I pray by now that that you have done an inquiry of yourself to remove all the hindrances of prayer as well as doing those things which would ensure that your prayers are going to be packed with power. You are going to see amazing results in your life of prayer

4

Accessing God

But know that the Lord has set apart for
Himself him who is godly; The Lord will
hear when I call to Him.
- Psalm 4:3

I want to share with you some valuable insights in you approaching God. To have successful prayer, specifically the prayer of supplication, you need to have a thorough understanding of approaching God when you pray. I'm not talking about kneeling or standing. I am not talking about those external factors, but I want you to grasp how that prayer that proceeds out of you will only have power to the degree that you know who you are and what is available to you. Many people lack confidence when they pray because they don't understand these vital components. If you lack confidence in prayer, your prayer will not produce much power.

YOUR NEW IDENTITY

The foundation of your prayer being answered is knowing that if you are a born-again believer that you are now the righteousness of God in Christ Jesus. When you were born again, you received a new identity. Paul tells us in 2 Corinthians 5:17, "If anyone is in Christ he is a new creation; old things have passed away; behold, all things have become new."

That identity now is that you are the righteousness of God in Christ Jesus. The answers to your prayers is not based upon your own righteousness, but solely on the righteousness of Jesus Christ. We often struggle with this because this is where satan fights us the most. How many times have you come to God in prayer for what you need only then to think about something that you are not doing right, or not living right? At that moment, satan attempts to persuade you into thinking that you are not qualified to even come to God in the first place. All my righteousness—according to God's word— is as filthy rags (Is. 64:6). Even your best state, according to God's standard of righteousness, still falls short. The apostle Paul states, "For all have sinned and fall short of the glory of God" (Rom. 3:23). If your prayers being answered were predicated upon your own righteousness, no one would get their prayers answered. Even our very salvation was based solely upon Him and not of us. Look at what Paul says in Romans 5:8, "But God demonstrates His own love toward us, in that while we were still sinners Christ died for us."

YOU ARE RIGHTEOUS

It is when we were completely without strength that Christ died for us. If we could do it ourselves, then we would not need a savior. It is because of the perfect sacrifice of Jesus Christ and being born in Him that you now have access. Don't ever think for a minute it is based upon your own righteousness. But to God be the glory, we have now traded in our rags of unrighteousness for His robe of righteousness. According to 2 Corinthians 5:21 the bible says, "For He made Him who knew no sin to be sin for us, that we might become the righteousness of God in Him."

The righteousness of God is a righteousness that comes from God. It is God's way of making a sinner right, or just, before Him. The word *'righteousness'* in Paul's letter to the Romans carries a double sense, and can be described as both legal and moral. In other words, the word refers to the legal actions God takes in declaring believers righteous, but it also refers to perfect righteousness, a characteristic that can only be attributed to God Himself in scripture and is the lofty standard for human behavior. This lofty standard cannot be achieved by anyone's effort, so God took the initiative to bring His people into a right relationship with Himself. We have now become the righteousness of God. Your identity was a gift and not based on your behavior. However, now your identify affects your behavior. He has now imputed his righteousness into your account and there is nothing satan can do about it. Jesus paid the price for your unrighteousness and gave you the gift of His righteousness. Look what Paul tells us in Romans 5:17, "For if by the one man's offense death reigned through the one, much more those who receive abundance of grace and of the gift of righteousness will reign in life through the One, Jesus Christ."

DECLARED NOT GUILTY

You and I are now the righteousness of God in Christ Jesus and there is nothing satan can do about it. If you go to God in prayer and satan or your carnal mind tries to persuade you that God is not going to hear your prayer, then do as I have done and use this powerful scripture.

Therefore, having been justified by faith, we have peace with God through our Lord Jesus Christ, through whom also we have access by faith into this grace in which we stand, and rejoice in hope of the glory of God. (Romans 5:1)

We have already been justified! That is past tense. You have already been justified. You are not going to be justified, but rather you were already justified by faith through our Lord Jesus Christ. Now to be justified means, "a one-time legal declaration stating not guilty." I remember someone saying it means, "Just-if-I had never sinned." That is the way God sees you now. You are not being justified—it's already done. God sees you now just as if you never sinned.

PEACE WITH GOD

Then the result of us being justified is that we have peace with God. It didn't just say the peace as in serenity and calmness, but rather you and I have peace with God. Because of man's sinful rebellions against God and His laws, the first great result of justification is that the sinner's war with God has ended forever. You have been reconciled to God; He is no longer against you.

For God was in Christ reconciling the world to Himself, not imputing their trespasses to them.

(2 Corinthians 5:19)

Even while you still have your issues that you are dealing with! If you have sinned, then confess your sin to Him because He is faithful and just to forgive you and cleanse you of all unrighteousness (1 Jn. 1:9).

ACCESS GRANTED

Then Paul goes on to say that, *"through whom"* (speaking of Jesus), we have access into this grace in which we stand. In addition to having peace with God, we also have through the work of Jesus Christ access to God into this new position of favor. To have access means, *"to approach"* as if by introduction into a king's throne. Believers have been granted admission to stand before God. Even though they were once rebels, they do not have to face His judgment. Instead, they approach His throne in the realm of grace, or in the King's favor. We have the freedom to enter His presence always. We have permission to approach God and communicate with God with freedom from fear. We are completely repositioned into a new realm of favor.

> **For we do not have a High Priest who cannot sympathize with our weaknesses, but was in all points tempted as we are, yet without sin. Let us therefore come boldly to the throne of grace that we may obtain mercy and find grace to help in time of need.**
>
> **(Hebrews 4:15-16)**

In the Old Testament, the high priest of Israel passed through the courts and veils into the Most Holy Place. Our High Priest has passed though the heavens to the very presence of God, where He sits at God's right hand. Jesus Christ is now our High Priest, representing us before God in heaven. Because our High Priest became flesh and lived here among earth, He now can sympathize with us. Jesus couldn't do this before because as the Word He did not understand what it was like to be tempted. He didn't understand what it was like to be hungry. He

45

didn't understand what it was like to be rejected, abandoned, lonely, or even feel grief. He had never experienced all these emotions we have here on earth. But because He became flesh, He can sympathize because He has shared those emotions with us. To sympathize means, *"to suffer with"*. It expresses the feeling of one who has entered suffering. When He took on the form of a man, he entered our suffering. Yet the one difference is that He experienced every degree of temptation, yet He never sinned. This is the beauty of Him being our High Priest. He is fully representing us before God because He now can share those intense emotions and feeling that we have and sympathize with us but also gives us the power to overcome.

Because we are now the righteousness of God, we can come boldly to the throne of grace. We don't have to be timid because of our past or failures. You can approach the King with confidence. You are going to obtain mercy, not judgment. You are going to find grace to help in time of need. It is our tendency when we are in need the most to run away from God. However, when you are in need you cannot afford to run from the throne of grace, but run to the throne of grace. When you come boldly to the throne of grace, you will obtain mercy and you are going to find every grace available when it is needed the most.

Therefore, brethren, having boldness to enter the Holiest by the blood of Jesus, by a new and living way which He consecrated

for us, through the veil, that is, His flesh, and having a High Priest over the house of God, let us draw near with a true heart in full assurance of faith having our hearts sprinkled form an evil conscience and our bodies washed with pure water.

(Hebrews 10: 19-22)

The scriptures call this a new and living way. In other words, this pathway into the Holy of Holies is a brand-new path. This pathway leads us into the very presence of God. It is not a pathway that has been slain with the blood of animals as in the Old Covenant, but with the precious blood of the lamb. Because of this, we can draw near in full assurance of faith. James tells us to "draw near to God, and He will draw near to you. Cleanse your hands, ye sinners; and purify your hearts you double minded" (Jam. 4:8). We can draw near to God in full assurance, with no doubt as to our acceptance when coming to God by the blood of Christ. Our faith and assurance is that the blood of Jesus has satisfied every requirement of God. Our assurance is not in ourselves, but in the finished work of Jesus Christ. This is important as it pertains to your life of prayer because the enemy is an accuser of the brethren. His assignment is to make you feel as though you are not accepted and God will not hear your prayer. Therefore, you need to have your mind renewed in this area. If the enemy can accuse you, then you will not be able to draw near, but rather you will withdraw. When you do that, you are not operating in faith.

YOU ARE ACCEPTED

You have been accepted not because of what you have done but because of what Christ has done on your behalf. Christ has made it possible for sinners to be accepted by God through the substitutionary death and imputed righteousness provided by Jesus Christ.

To the praise of the glory of His grace, by which he made us accepted in the Beloved.
(Ephesians 1:6-7)

You could not make yourself accepted. He made you acceptable. Your acceptance is not based on your performance. Your acceptance is based on what Christ has done for you. What had once caused us to be rejected we have not been made accepted. Christ has made you accepted. There is nothing you can do to make yourself more accepted than the finished work of Christ.

DEVELOPING BOLDNESS

Boldness is not a natural attribute, especially when it comes to coming to God in prayer. Boldness is a result of knowing who you are in Christ, your identity. Once you have a firm foundation of your identity through the word of God you, this is a great way to begin your prayer by being thankful for a very important person that God has made, you. It is so easy to get caught in the trap of satan that suggests that you are not worthy, not righteousness, and that you have no access to God. Speak the words of God out loud. Your access to the throne of God and your position as the righteousness of God in Christ Jesus is not based upon your feelings, but what God has already said about you in the word of God. Your boldness is not determined by your emotions, but rather by faith in God's Word. The times that I have had prayers answered the most is not when I was feeling emotionally strong, but I had to have confidence in His Word even when I wasn't feeling I deserved it Paul tells the church in Ephesians 3:12, "In whom we have boldness and access with confidence by the faith in Him."

God wants you to have boldness in your prayer. You have access, and that access has been given to you to exercise with boldness. You need to get these scriptures in your spirit. Develop your inner life in prayer. As you meditate upon these guidelines, your inner life will be built up, and you will begin to develop boldness and authority.

Love has been perfected among us in this: that we may have boldness in the day of judgment: because as He is, so are we in this world. (1John 4:17)

As Christ is right now, this is how God sees you. As Christ is righteous, so are you in this world. As

Christ is accepted, so are you in this world. As Christ is holy, so are you in this world. Your identity is the foundation for your life as a believer and especially in your life of prayer. Your prayer of supplication will be more effective as you are rooted in your identity. Battles are won and lost in this area. Even satan came to Jesus to question his identity by saying, *"...if you are the son of God."* Christ knew beyond a shadow of a doubt who He was, and you need to know who you are as well. You are righteous. You have been justified. You are accepted. You have access. You have boldness. You can have true assurance of faith.

5

The Pathway to Prayer

*I beseech you therefore brethren, by the mercies of
God that you present your bodies a living sacrifice,
holy, acceptable to God which is your reasonable
service*
- Romans 12:1

Now that God has illuminated your mind with the
truth of your identity. Understanding your identity
will now affect your behavior as well as your prayer
life. If you want to be a person who sees your prayers
of supplication answered more often, then you must
become a worshiper.

**Now we know that God does not hear
sinners; but if anyone is a worshiper of God
and does His will, He hears him.**

(John 9:31)

Being a worshiper of God is pivotal in having your
prayer of supplication answered. Have you ever

heard people pray and ask God for something and they are not even a believer? People try to bargain and negotiate with God all the time. If you want to capture God's attention become a worshiper. He listens to worshipers. Worshipers are those who do God's will. So, then the question is not do you go to church, but are you a worshiper? If God only hears the worshipers, then we must understand what a worshiper is.

In today's churches, it is very customary to sing a couple of up-tempo songs, which we call "praise." Then, oftentimes the team slows down the tempo, which is generally called "worship." This is why we use the term "praise and worship."

However, I believe that being a worshiper goes beyond what tempo of song a person is singing, or if they are singing at all. Being a worshiper has nothing to do with music or singing. Although it may involve music, the essential nature of worship is not found in singing. God does not hear you just because you sing songs to Him. That is not what qualifies you as a worshiper. A worshiper is a person that worships God by giving a sacrifice. Under the Old Covenant, the people brought different sacrifices to God as an act of worship. Those sacrifices were animals that were slain and then offered up to God as an expression of devotion. Under the New Covenant, we do not bring sacrificial animals to God as an act of devotion but we offer up ourselves as a sacrifice to God as an act of devotion. This is something you do willingly.

I beseech you therefore, brethren, by the mercies of God, that you present your bodies a living sacrifice, holy, acceptable to God which is your reasonable service.

(Romans. 12:1)

Paul is saying that in view of all the mercy that God has shown towards you that your spiritual act of worship is to present yourself as a living sacrifice. When you offer yourself to God as a living sacrifice, a living gift to God, you are worshiping God. When you worship God and you become a living sacrifice, you no longer live for yourself but for Him. God is looking for worshipers. He is actively seeking worshipers.

But the hour is coming and now is, when the true worshipers will worship the Father in spirit and truth; for the Father is seeking such to worship Him. God is Spirit and those who worship Him must worship in spirit and truth. (John 4:23-24)

Worship is a matter of the heart. If you want to see tremendous results in prayer, it is essential that you be a worshiper. You can go to church every Sunday but still not be a worshiper. You can sing on the praise team but that doesn't mean you are worshiper. Being a worshiper means that you are living in a way that is pleasing to God. You are not seeking your own will but you are seeking to live in agreement with His word. When God finds a worshiper, His ears are open to their cry. The book of 2 Chronicles 16:9 says, "For the eyes of the Lord run to and fro throughout the whole earth, to show Himself strong on behalf of those who heart is loyal to Him."

The eyes of the Lord are scanning the earth looking for worshipers whose hearts are loyal to him. When God finds those whose hearts are devoted to Him, He will show Himself strong on your behalf. He is looking for people that have a loyal heart so He can bring a divine interruption into your situation to manifest His power. Paul states, "I beseech you therefore, brethren, by the mercies of God, that you present your bodies a living sacrifice, holy, acceptable to God, which is your reasonable service" (Rom.12:1).

Now that you see that for your prayers to be heard, it is required to be a worshiper. A worshiper is required to bring a sacrifice. Under the Old Covenant, God accepted the sacrifices of dead animals. But because of Christ's ultimate sacrifice, the Old Covenant sacrifices are no longer in effect (Heb.9:11-12). For those in Christ, the only acceptable worship is to offer themselves completely to the Lord. You must completely yield to Him as an instrument of righteousness. This is your spiritual act of worship. Because of what God has done for us, we owe God our highest form of service. This is the least we can do. This is a daily surrender, yielding to Him. God will not do it for us; it is our responsibility to present ourselves. Our motive for obedience is the mercy of God. This is where we voluntarily submit to every change God wants to bring in our lives. We release control of our lives to God. It is a willingness that is found in trust in Him with our lives. God doesn't want your stuff, He wants you! Your heart, your mind, your soul, your thoughts, your devotion, your eyes, your ears, your will. Presenting yourself to God is practically lived out through grateful obedience. Our worship is our response to His generous mercy.

We have just seen how God has positioned us into a place where we can connect with Him through prayer. You need to have a revelation of who you are in God so when you come to God's throne, it is your understanding of your identity that is going to give you boldness.

I want to share with you a very simple guide to prayer. Remember prayer is not a formula. Nevertheless, there are times when we need some guidance. Have you ever been at a place in your life when you come to Him and you just start bombarding God with all your issues? I know I have. I am not saying that God will not hear you, but I think that most of those prayers are not offered up in faith and they are stress releasers rather than incense of prayers. Your prayers must be fueled with faith. You must get in faith. You must get Gods attention because you need the ear of God. So, let's look at a very simple strategy that has worked for many. It's a great tool when you need a little assistance.

THE A.C.T.S. METHOD

Experiencing Transformative Prayer

I have found that there are movements to experiencing transformative prayer. As you progress through these various movements of prayer you will begin to see that your prayer will become more diversified. Utilizing this orderly sequence will assist you when your problems seem to overwhelm you. This pattern is a very simple sequence that can remember that will bring tremendous fulfillment in your prayer life. Let's begin to look at this pattern.

A- *Adoration*

Adoration is extremely vital in your prayer life. You cannot bypass spending a few moments adoring who God is. Adoration sets the tone for the entire prayer. It reminds us whom we are addressing, whose presence we have entered, whose attention we have gained. Many people want to just give God a list without taking that time to acknowledge who He is. I have found that when I take the time to adore God, it takes the focus off me and my and puts it now on Him. When you begin to do that, you will see that your problems will begin to be minimized as God is maximized.

Adoration reminds us of God's identity and inclination. When we make mention of God's attributes, lifting His character and personality, we reinforce our understanding of who He is. When you are worshipping Him for being faithful, righteous, just, merciful, gracious, and recognizing His willingness to provide, you are worshipping Him in truth for who He is and not just what He has done. You should find yourself standing in awe of this incredible gift that God has lavished His love on us and that we are now His children.

Our God is omnipotent, omniscient, omnipresent, and yet loves and watches over us. There is no better way to adore God than list his attributes. I like to focus on one attribute depending on what my circumstance may be. For instance, If I am facing a major decision, I locate scriptures that focus on His guidance. When I am in financial need, then I worship him for his provision, power, and providence. Some of the best-known psalms are Psalm 8,19,23,46,95,100, and 148. Adoring God is like breathing: you cannot live without it. When you find yourself standing in the presence of a Holy God you cannot help but surrender to Him. This is the heart of a worshiper.

C- Confession

Now that you have entered the presence of a Holy God through worship this is a prime opportunity to acknowledge those areas of your life that do not reflect him. Your prayers will not be effective if you still have areas in your life that are contrary to His will that you have not confessed to God. During this moment in your prayer time, ask God to search and reveal to you those areas that have been unconfessed. David prayer in Psalm 139:23-24

Search me, O God, and know my heart; try me, and know my anxieties: And see if there be any wicked way in me, and lead me in the way everlasting

There are times when it doesn't take God long to search and reveal those things in your heart and mind. They are right on the surface. However, there are other times when you need to allow God to go deep into the chambers of your heart and mind and reveal those hidden, protected areas that He wants you to confess. Give the Holy Spirit time to do this. Do not rush through this time. He is the revealer. He will reveal to you the area in which you are unaware of that may be blocking you from getting your prayers answered. Once the Holy Spirit reveals those things, immediately confess them and thank Him for forgiveness.

T- Thanksgiving
We need to develop and attitude that expresses thanksgiving to God. Not just in our minds, but giving God verbal thanks for specific things that He has done in our lives. Let me share with you what I call the prescription for thanksgiving.

Bless the Lord O my soul; and all that is within me, bless his holy name. Bless the LORD. O my soul, and forget not all his benefits: Who forgives all your iniquities, Who heals all your diseases, Who redeems

your life from destruction, Who crowns you with lovingkindness and tender mercies, Who satisfies your mouth with good things, So that your youth is renewed like the eagle's. (Psalm 103:1-5)

This was a Psalm of David, and he makes a very interesting statement on what he is grateful for. David says that he will not forget all his benefits. You and I have benefits. When you work for a company many times they may give you benefits which may include paid vacation, a retirement plan, and health insurance. These benefits are the advantages that you have because you are a part of an organization. As a child of God, you and I have benefits. Our benefits are a result of our covenant with God. David lists five specific benefits that he was going to bless the Lord for. Five is the number for grace and favor. These are our benefits of our covenant of grace.

5 Benefits of Our Covenant

1. Forgiveness
> **...Who forgives all your iniquities**

We have the benefit of being forgiven of all our sins and iniquities because of the blood of Jesus Christ. Because we are in Christ we have redemption, you have redemption now. He has already provided the blood necessary to bring you to God. Paul states, **"In Him we have redemption through His blood, the**

forgiveness of sins, according to the riches of His grace" (Eph. 1:7). Take the time to thank God for the blood of Jesus and the forgiveness you have in Him.

2. Healing
...Who heals all your diseases

Our God is a healer. There is no sickness, no disease that God is not able to heal. If there has ever been a time in your life that God has healed you emotionally, physically, or mentally, you should continue to give God thanks. Healing is part of your covenant rights as a child of God.

But He was wounded for our transgressions, He was bruised for our iniquities: The chastisement for our peace was upon Him, and by His stripes we are healed. (Isaiah 53:5)

3. Redemption
...Who redeems your life from destruction

God is a redeemer. To redeem means to buy back and bring back. His blood paid the price for you. You belong to Him. As a result, He is going to redeem you from all your destruction. The enemy is a destroyer. He comes to steal, kill, and destroy (John 10:10). You have an adversary that is out to destroy your purpose, destiny, life, money, relationships, and dreams.

No weapon formed against you will prosper, and every tongue which rises up against you in judgment You shall condemn. This is the heritage of the servants of the Lord. (Isaiah 54:17)

This is your heritage, your benefit. God can redeem my life from satan, but I also have found out that I have a lot of self-destructive patterns and behaviors in my own life that God will redeem me from. Sometimes satan didn't need any help; I was doing a good job with my own destructive thinking, and behaving. But thank God that He has redeemed me from myself! Give God thanks that He has redeemed you from destruction. Many of us have experienced destructive patterns of behavior in our lives, but God's hand can go down to the farthest pit and bring us out.

He also brought me up out of a horrible pit, Out of the miry clay, and set my feet upon a rock, and established my steps. He has put a new song in my mouth- Praise to our God. (Psalm 40:2-3)

4. Protection

...Who crowns you with lovingkindness and tender mercies

After God brings you out of the pit of destruction, He crowns you with loving-kindness and tender mercies. The word for loving-kindness refers to God's gracious love. It is a comprehensive term that encompasses love, grace, mercy, goodness, forgiveness, truth, compassion, and faithfulness. The Hebrew word for *"crown"* carries the idea of encircling for protection. When we put these together, we see that God is going to literally encircle you and encase you with His love, grace, mercy, goodness, forgiveness, truth, compassion, and faithfulness. These are going to become a protective barrier in your life.

> **This I recall to my mind; therefore, have I hope. It is of the LORD'S mercies that we are not consumed because His compassion's fail not. They are new every morning: great is your faithfulness.**
> **(Lamentations 3:21-23)**

There are times when you can get forgetful and you need to recall past times that God has been good to you. Hope begins to spring forth in your heart when you rehearse past victories that God has demonstrated faithfulness. The prophet states that the only reason that he was not consumed is because God's mercies and compassion never failed. Not only do they never fail, but they are new every morning. You will never be able to completely exhaust the lovingkindness of God. Every morning there is fresh mercy, fresh love, and fresh grace awaiting you.

5. Fulfillment

..Who satisfies your mouth with good things

God will satisfy our mouth with good things. There is a hunger in the soul of man that only God can fill. No man has ever filled to satisfaction but a believer, and only God Himself can satisfy him. Only God can satisfy the hunger and craving in the heart of man. The good that the Lord bestows upon us is not vain worldly toys and pleasures, but the satisfaction of Him.

Each of these benefits is in a progressive order. You move from being forgiven, to being healed, from healed to redeemed, from redeemed to crowned, and then to being satisfied. As you begin to give God thanks for all these tremendous benefits, you will see that your life in prayer will begin to soar and take on new life. Not only does God bless you the benefits of the covenant, but every day your account is being loaded with benefits. David tells us, "Blessed be the Lord, who daily loads us with benefits, even the God of our salvation" (Ps. 68:19). God daily loads us with these benefits. Every day, there are benefits awaiting you. This requires us to thank God for all He has done for us.

S-*Supplication*

Now that you have adored him, confessed your sins, and thanked Him for all His benefits, you are now ready to ask Him what you need. We all have needs. This is where you are getting heaven involved into the affairs on the earth. When you put your needs before God, you are acknowledging who He is, and that He is your source for your provision. You can easily break down your needs into various categories which may include family, finances, personal relationships, and ministry. After you have thanked God for what He has already done in your life, you will begin to sense your faith elevate. You can borrow the faith and strength of previous victories to sustain you in a present time of need.

6

Preparing Your Case

*See now, I have prepared my case, I know
that I shall be vindicated*

-Job 13:18

It is very easy when you find yourself in an urgent situation or need to pray what I call "911" prayers. Your prayers are rooted in anxiety and desperation rather than faith, and without faith, it is impossible to please God.

One way to ensure that you do not fall into this pattern of prayer is to take the time to construct a prayer of supplication. I want to share some insights with you that I have found beneficial in constructing a prayer of supplication. These are not rules that you have follow; however, you may find that it will help provide a sense of direction to keep you on track so that you are not allowing the emotions to dictate your prayer.

One of the first things that I have found extremely helpful is to have a prayer journal. The journal will serve as a spiritual map. It will provide to you reference points from previous times that God has answered your prayer. This will give you a sense of confidence because if God has done it previously, He is more than able and willing to do it again. I love it when I have a prayer that has been written down, and then I can check it off, and date when God has answered my prayers. Another reason that I believe it is important to write down your prayer is that it shows God that this situation is important to you. There is something about taking the time to write down your prayer and do the work before you even bring your petitions to God in the first place.

As we begin to construct our petition, it is important to put the date next to your requests when you presented this to God. We cannot put God on a timeline however, you will begin to see the workings of God in your life, and it will reveal your journey with God.

The prayer of supplication conveys the idea of approaching God for a favor. In other words, you are requesting something. The specific request, or favor you are seeking is called a petition. In the prayer of supplication, you may have several petitions, or requests. In the world of government or business, a petition is an official document that is addressed to a person in authority or power, soliciting some favor, aid, or other benefit. If you are going to draw up an official document to bring it to an individual, then you should take the time to prepare it.

If your need, favor, or request is that important to you, then wouldn't it make sense to take the time necessary to construct a prayer of supplication to bring it before the high court of heaven, the supreme authority over all and perform a kingdom transaction? Job 13:18 says; See now, I have prepared my case, I know that I shall be vindicated. (Job 13:18)

Job says that he prepared his case. You need to take the time to prepare your case. Suppose you were scheduled to go to court for an auto accident claim. You hired your lawyer, you paid his retainer, and you gave him everything that he requested. On the day of your hearing, he walks in and tells you that he didn't take the time to prepare your case. You could have had thousands of dollars coming to you, but because of his lack of preparation, you were not awarded the money. This is how many people treat prayer. They have things coming to them, but they never take the time to prepare their case and they leave things up to chance.

What does it take to prepare your case? You need to take the time to gather your evidence and get your witnesses in place. What evidence are you going to submit to the highest authority? This is where you go through the Word of God and you find your covenant promises and write them down. The Holy Spirit will reveal to you God's promises so that you can come to God in faith. Get as much evidence as you need to support your argument of why this should be granted. Write it out, and submit it to God through prayer.

Now this is the confidence that we have in Him, that if we ask any thing according to His will, He hears us. And if we know that He hears us, whatever we ask, we know that we have the petitions that we have asked of Him. (1 John 5:14)

Scripture tells us that if we ask anything that is according to Gods will we have those petitions. So, the key is to getting your requests answered is making sure that what you are asking for agrees with the will of God. You may say, "I'm not sure if it is the will of God?" The written word of God is the revealed will of God for your life. Healing is the will of God. Peace is the will of God. Financial provision is the will of God. If your request can be found in God's Word, then that is His will for your life. Your petition is founded in the Word of God.

Your petition that you have written up is a legal document that you are filing into the courts of heaven. You are standing in the authority of Christ, using His name, His authority, using His Word with confidence, boldness and assurance.

It is amazing what you will learn about people's prayer lives when you listen to them pray. One thing that I have observed is that many people thank God for things that they have never asked for. The bible declares that we have not because we ask not. In other words, one reason that people never receive is that they never asked God in the first place. I have heard people say, "God, I thank you for the new job."

It's good to thank God for answered prayer before you receive an answer. However, you need to be specific: you asked God for a job, but not the type of job you want. Yes, God already knows what you have need of before you ask Him, but that does not release you from the responsibility of asking Him. There are so many passages of scripture that pertain to asking God for what we need. It seems so trivial, but so many people don't receive because they never asked in the first place. Observe the following scriptures and see how important it is in asking.

And whatever things you ask in prayer, believing, you will receive. (Matthew 21:22)

If you abide in Me, and My words abide in you, you will ask what you desire, and it shall be done for you. (John 15:7)

Are you beginning to get the picture? Asking God for what we need is extremely important. Don't assume that just because God already knows what you need without asking Him, that you are going to receive.

For the believer, prayer is a legal claim on your covenant rights, you cannot be passive about this, God has given you the authority to put a demand of something due. You are not demanding God, but you are placing a claim on His provision. Therefore, it is imperative that you know your covenant rights as a believer.

Jesus states that if His words abide in us, we will

ask what we desire and it shall be done. He is not giving us a blank check on what we want. When His word is in us, then our desires will align with His. Then when we ask, our asking is in direct alignment with His word. Therefore, it shall be done.

And this is the confidence that we have in him, that if we ask any thing according to his will, he hears us: And if we know that he hears us , whatsoever we ask, we know that we have the petitions that we desired of him (1 John 5: 15-16)

Therefore, we can have confidence. Our confidence is the based upon His will. His will is His Word that is abiding in us. When His Word is abiding in us, then our desires will be meshed with His desires. We then take our desires and form them into a prayer of supplication. That prayer of supplication is rooted in God awakening a desire within us because of His Word. God is the one who puts the desire in us in the first place in order that we would ask him in prayer so He can give us what He wants us to have. We are going to look a scripture that many of us know, and you may even have it memorized, and have quoted it, but you have not received the revelation of it so that it can become a reality.

So Jesus answered and said to them, "Have faith in God. For assuredly, I say to you, whoever says to this mountain, Be removed

**and be cast into the sea, and does not doubt
in his heart, but believes that those things
which he says will be done, he will have
whatever he says. Therefore I say to you,
Whatever things you ask when you pray,
believe that you receive them, and you will
have them. (Mark 11:22-24)**

We are to have faith in God constantly. How do
we have faith in God? Well, faith comes by hearing
God's Word (Rom.10:17). He tells us that there is so
much power in faith filled words that even a
mountain must obey.

**Now faith is the substance of things hoped
for, the evidence of things not seen.
(Hebrews 11:1)**

The word *"substance"* is *"hupostasis"* in the Greek.
It carries the meaning of confidence, assurance, or
title-deed. A title-deed is proof of ownership. Your
faith is your title-deed. Where does that faith come
from? It comes from God's word. When you received
your promise from God's word faith came with it.
Your faith is the title deed, proof of ownership, of
what you are hoping for.

Jesus say's, "the words that I speak to you are
spirit, and they are life" (Jn. 6:63). God's words are
spiritual in nature. His words are also life. This word
for *"life"* is *"zoe."* It is the highest form of life. It is the
life that God has, it is His life. His Words are spirit in

nature and they carry the *zoe* of God, the God kind of life. They have a creative ability when spoken by a believer.

What things soever ye desire, when ye pray, believe that ye receive them, and ye shall have them. (Mark 11:24 KJV)

Jesus teaches us to ask for what we desire. He is referring to the desires in us because of God's word abiding in you. Jesus wants us to be at the level of spiritual maturity so that God's word is so ingrained in your heart, that your desire is his desire. Most of us of us are not there yet, so few of our desires are God's desires, and our prayers seem unanswered.

Receiving from God doesn't take place after you pray. You must believe that you received when you prayed. This is one thing that many people don't understand. It is easy to believe once you have it, but you must believe that you received it when you prayed.

Once you prayed that prayer of supplication with all your supporting evidence and you put a demand on something that is due, based upon the revealed will of God, then there will be an assurance in your spirit that you received it now. There is an internal knowing that even though you don't see it yet, you know you have received it. There is an unshakable confident expectation in your spirit that you received it.

However, many people miss out on their

manifestation because they do not understand the difference between receiving and having. There is a distinction between receiving and having. To *receive* means you have taken possession of it in your spirit, your inner man. *Having* means you now have possession of it in its manifested form. So, *having* is the manifestation of what you received in your spirit by faith. Notice that you believed you received it when you prayed, which is present tense. However, it then states you *shall have* them. This speaks of something in the future. This is what I call, " *already but not yet.*"

Let me give you an example of what I mean so that this may help you. Let's say that I have a friend who needs a car. I have shown him a picture of a car that I have that I am willing to give him, but until he asks, I don't know if he wants it or not. He asks for the car after he has seen a picture of it. I then go to my office and get the title out and sign it over to his name. He is now the proud owner of my car. He is so excited, that he finally got a car. He no longer must ask for a ride or take the bus to work. However, the car is at my house. The title demonstrates proof of ownership. He is now the owner of a car. He *received* ownership of the car when I gave him the title. However, he does not yet *have* possession the car yet, because it is still in my garage. In between *receiving* and *having* is a period called time. You see, many people don't realize that there is time between receiving and having. Let's look at how to navigate during the time between receiving and having.

7

The Art of Waiting

Cast not away therefore your confidence, which hath great recompense of reward. For ye have need of patience, that, after ye have done the will of God, you might receive the promise.
-Hebrews 10:35-36 KJV

I realize that when we come to God we want everything right now. We need a breakthrough as of yesterday. There are times when God releases things suddenly in our lives. However, most of the time our answers to prayer take longer than we like. We need to understand the laws of the realm of the spirit and the natural. Learning how to respond to those periods of waiting will help facilitate your breakthrough.

It is during this season that it appears that nothing is happening. Waiting for answers to come can seem so frustrating. Waiting is no fun at all, especially when there are things trying to pressure you. This waiting period is where your faith will be tested while you are waiting for the manifestation of your promise. What you do during this time while you are waiting for your manifestation is crucial.

The manifestation of your prayer will often take time to come into materiality. This is receiving the end of your faith. However, during this period of time, you cannot afford to get weak in faith. When you came out of prayer, your faith was strong, it was high. As time passes, it is very easy to get discouraged.

Waiting on God in faith does not mean passively sitting around, but being actively engaged with Him and His movements. Waiting entails a confident expectation and actively hoping in the Lord. Waiting is never a passive resignation but it is an active waiting. The word *"wait"* literally means, *"to bind together by twisting."* It is like braiding a rope. When you are waiting, you are interweaving and winding yourself around His presence and promises. While you are waiting, you are binding yourself with God to such a degree that His power, His strength is being fused into your inner man. This is what Isaiah had in mind when he wrote,

Have you not known? Have you not heard? The everlasting God, the LORD, The Creator of the ends of the earth, neither faints nor is weary. His understanding is unsearchable. He gives power to the weak, and to those who have no might He increases strength. Even the youths shall faint and be weary, and the you men shall utterly fall, but those who wait

on the Lord Shall renew their strength; They shall mount up with wings like eagles, They shall run and not be weary, They shall walk and not faint.

(Isaiah 40:28-31)

Our faith must be founded upon the credibility and faithfulness of God. God never faints; He is never weary. He is never too exhausted to meet the demands of His people. God is not too weak to act on behalf of His people. Even though the young and strong eventually become tired and fall, the Ancient of Days never does. Not only does He "not faint," but He gives power to them who do faint. Those that have no strength in themselves have strength in Him, and He increases that strength. The criterion of receiving God's unlimited strength is waiting upon the Lord. While you are waiting, you will be transformed. Eventually, you are going to renew your strength and mount up with wings as eagles. This depicts a spiritual transformation that faith brings to a person.

Be not weary in well doing: for in due season we shall reap, if we faint not
(Galatians 6:9)

Paul admonished the church not to get tired in the process of waiting for their harvest. He understood that people have the propensity to give up, be discouraged, and throw in the towel of faith if the answer seems prolonged.

Weariness just doesn't happen one day when you wake up in the morning. Weariness grows when you begin to loosen your grip of faith. Once weariness starts to grow, fatigue sets in, fatigue turns into hopelessness, and can even lead to depression. Don't lose your grip; let your grip of faith grow stronger every day! You must guard your heart from allowing weariness to grow.

During this period of waiting, you need to know that your faith is going to be tested. I never liked tests in school and I don't like them today. However, tests are a part of our spiritual development and maturing process. The testing process usually occurs through trials.

My brethren, count it all joy when you fall into various trials, knowing that the testing of your faith produces patience. But let patience have its perfect work, that you may be perfect and complete, lacking nothing.

(James 1:2-3)

Trials are of outward circumstances. They are conflicts, sufferings, and troubles that are encountered by all believers. Trials are not pleasant and may be extremely grievous, but believers are to consider them as opportunities for rejoicing. Troubles and difficulties are a tool, which refines and purifies our faith producing patience and endurance.

The testing of your faith means, *"proving the*

authenticity." It was a term used for the process to determine whether coins were genuine and not. The purpose of testing is not to destroy, but to purge and refine all impurities out of precious metals, so finally proving to be authentic. Your faith will be tested. Even Abraham's faith had to be tested.

The result of your faith being tested is that it is going to produce patience. Usually, when we hear the word patience, we think of something that is going to take a long, long, long time. However, I realize that patience is not standardized. How long is patient? Let me show you what I mean. In every culture, every nation, time is standardized. Everywhere, one day is 24 hours. That is standardized, whether you live in a third world country or in New York City. One hour is 60 minutes. One minute is composed of 60 seconds. If you tell someone I will be there is 2 minutes, then regardless of his background, he knows that in 120 seconds you will return. However, you may ask him to be patient. Patience may have nothing to do with time. The word patience implies the idea of "standing fast under pressure, with a staying power that turns adversity into opportunity." You don't let the pressure get you out of faith. You learn to stand fast under pressure with a staying power. While you are standing fast, you can turn your greatest adversity into your greatest opportunity.

We need to learn stop complaining and begin rejoicing. One of the issues that kept the children of Israel in the wilderness for so long is they were always complaining. So, when you stop complaining and start to count it all joy, you literally begin to shift yourself out of a season of waiting and you can begin to position yourself so that you will see opportunities that will assist you for the manifestation of your prayers in your life.

Abraham received a promise that took 25 years to manifest. Talk about faith being tested! However, in that 25 years, his faith was never weak. He did not stagger at God's promise. He never acted with hesitation; he grew strong in faith. If anyone has a right to be weary and faint, it would be Abraham.

And being not weak in faith, he did not consider his own body, already dead (since was about a hundred years old), and the deadness of Sarah's womb. He did not at the promise of God through unbelief; but was strengthened in faith, giving glory to God; and being fully convinced that, what He had promised He was able also to perform. (Romans 4:19-21)

We need to look at some of the keys that caused his faith to get stronger as he waited on the Lord. Despite his age—Abraham was ninety-nine years old— he believed that God would bring forth the promise. Secondly, Abraham continued to give glory to God. His faith grew as he gave God the glory, which now caused him to be completely, and fully persuaded. Nothing could talk him out of it.

Hebrews 6:15 states; **"And so after he had patiently endured he obtained the promise."**

He continued to worship, honor, and praise God. The more he glorified God, the more his faith grew, and as his faith grew, he became fully persuaded. This is what you do while you are waiting. Thank God for what you have already received even when you don't have it yet. Giving God glory through thanksgiving is evidence that what I believed I received is on the way.

> **Do not become sluggish, but imitate those who through faith and patience inherit the promises. (Hebrews 6:12)**

We need to follow the example of those that preceded us. If it took faith and patience to obtain the promises of God, then that is what it is going got take for us as well. Faith and patience are inseparable is it pertains to you obtaining the manifestation of your prayer.

> **Therefore, do not cast away your confidence, which has great reward. For ye have need of endurance, so that after you have done the will of God, you might receive the promise. (Hebrews 10:35-36)**

Do not throw away the confidence that comes from God's words to you. It is during this time that you must stand and believe God despite what you see with your natural eye. Your confidence is not in the arm of flesh, but your confidence is in the absoluteness of God's unchanging word. No matter what happens, continue to remember your reward. Act like you are already living it. Keep on patiently doing God's will if you want Him to do for you all that he has promised. Don't stop doing the right things!

8

Laws of Manifestation

*By faith we understand that the worlds were
framed by the word of God, so that things which
are seen were not made of things which are visible*
-Hebrews 11:3

Before we get into some very practical things that
we can do to cooperate with God, I want to share
with you some truths concerning the realm of the
spirit so that we understand what is taking place,
then we can be intentional with practical actions that
will correspond with what we are believing for. Just
as there are laws that govern our natural world, there
are also laws that govern the realm the spirit. The
world of the spirit is a very real world. It is invisible
to the naked eye, but visible through the eyes of faith.
There is spiritual activity that is presently taking
place around you.

Earlier, we discussed that the words that Jesus
spoke were spirit and life (Jn. 6:63). The words

themselves were spirit in nature. They find their origin in God and since God is Spirit, His Words are spiritual. Since God spoke everything into existence, all of creation has its origin in God's spiritual words.

By faith we understand that the worlds were framed by the word of God, so that things which are seen were not made of things which are visible. (Hebrews 11:3)

The writer of Hebrews says that through faith we understand that the worlds, the stars the planets, in fact all things were made at God's command. When God gave the command, they were framed. God first created the heavens, which is the world of the spirit and then the earth, constructed of matter. So, everything that we can see now, did not come into existence from other things that previously existed. Everything that exists today finds its origin in God in the realm of the spirit.

When you constructed your prayer of supplication and you found your evidence through the scriptures and when you asked in faith and put claim on something that is due, you were not using your own words, you were using God's words. It is your voice, but His Word. Since you were using God's words, the natures of those words are spirit and life. When you prayed, your words went into the spirit realm and it began to "frame your world."

Now faith is the substance of things hoped

for, the evidence of things not seen.

(Hebrews 11:1)

Your faith, which came through hearing God's Word, is the evidence of something you cannot see presently with the naked eye. It's invisible because it is still being framed. The moment you spoke God's words, even though you don't see anything happening in natural realm, you have just activated a great amount of activity in the realm of the spirit, where now things are being arranged that is congruent to what you spoke.

There is a conversion process that takes place between the spirit world and the natural world. The Word is spiritual, but what you need is natural. You will not be able to pay your automobile payment by just quoting to your banker Philippians 4:19. However, when you prayed, "My God shall supply all your need according to His riches in glory," you just released spiritual words that are now going forth to frame, create, and convert those spiritual words until you receive the physical manifestation for what you need.

So shall My word be that goes forth out of my mouth: It shall not return unto Me void, But it shall accomplish what I please, and it shall prosper in the thing for which I sent it. (Isaiah 55:11)

Based upon this verse, God says that it is impossible for His Word to go out and return void.

That word cannot turn back, or retreat. It cannot return empty or ineffective. That word now must be accomplished, fulfilled, and it will prosper. Most people don't realize that when they speak Gods words, they become the mouthpiece of God in the earth. When you speak God's words, in the name of Jesus Christ, God is speaking through you. That is why Jesus says whatever you ask in my name, I will do it.

In the realm of the spirit, time does not exist. Everything is in the now. When you speak the word, you are releasing a force that originates in the spirit realm packed with creativity that is now being superimposed into the natural world. Let me share with you in my testimony how this worked.

I needed a financial miracle, The Holy Spirit said, "Let me teach you how to pray the money in your life you need." That is when I began to learn about the prayer of supplication. I went through Gods Word and gathered my evidence. I prepared my case. I presented my request to God. While I was praying, I believed that I had received the money by faith. Did I have it? No, but I believed that I had received it. Where did I receive it? In my spirit. When did I receive it? When I prayed, which happened to be on the 1st day of the month. I believed that I had received it, but I didn't have it. I released God's promises, which are spirit and life, those words went forth and converted and framed my money I needed. On day 2, I thanked God for what I already received in my spirit. In prayer on day 3, I again thanked God for what I received. The evidence was not in my bank account, but the evidence was my faith. Now here is what is so amazing about the whole thing. I had several ministry assignments that I had scheduled that month, but suddenly, I got calls from those engagements that needed to reschedule for a later date.

My faith was now beginning to go through a trial to see if I believed what I received. It was testing time. Well, I will never forget the initial breakthrough. I was ministering in Washington, D.C., and after service, a young man ran up to me and gave me a small envelope. I thanked him and went back to the office to be refreshed. I didn't pay that much attention to the envelope. Outwardly, the young man didn't look like he even had money to catch a bus home. When I got to the hotel room, I remembered the envelope and unfolded it, and to my amazement, there was $1000. I was stunned. That taught me never to look at how people may appear. I went to my next assignment and the same thing happens again. Remember, I told you that my schedule was being drastically reduced. Yet, God began to tell me that when it looks like the enemy is decreasing you, I am in the process of increasing you. I then went to my next assignment and to my amazement an individual I had ministered to said they felt led to sow $1000. My faith was beginning to soar. I had another ministry engagement and the Lord spoke to another individual to sow $3000 to me. This was just the beginning, in just a few weeks I had all the money that I needed for my circumstance.

It would have been just as easy for God to have it automatically deposited supernaturally in my bank account, yet it took 30 days because I had to go to the designated places in which He already commanded people to be a part of what that word I prayed to take on form. You see when it doesn't look like God is moving, doesn't mean He is not working. Sometimes God is lining people up, and making connections, and setting up appointments to get you in the right position for what you prayed for to take place. When you pray using God's Word your answer is in the process of being framed, it is taking on form.

Ask, and it will be given you; seek, and you will find; knock, and it will be opened unto you; For everyone asks receives; and he who seeks finds; and to him who knocks it will be opened. (Matthew 7:7-8)

Jesus is describing a sequential process for prayer. Three words imply distinct degrees of intensity. First, there is the *"asking."* Then, *"seeking"* and finally, the *"knocking."* When you asked in faith, at that moment you believed that you had received from God. After you come out of the closet of prayer, you begin to seek, acting as if you have received what you asked for. You are acting on your prayer of faith. The promise is that what we ask and seek shall be given us. If you asked for a new job and believe that you have received it, then you cannot seek while you are sitting on the sofa watching television. It is less likely that you will receive a job without first seeking for a job. Sometimes, when you ask, what you receive is direction. You received a connection to your next step, which will ultimately place you on the correct path, putting you in front of the people that can make it happen for you. Once the Spirit leads me to the door, I can then knock and it shall be opened. Doors of opportunity to be opened that will release what you asked for. If it doesn't open, I go back to see where I may have missed it in my seeking.

I am in the process, of asking, seeking, and knocking I am also continuing to speak my confession of faith based upon the Word of God. This is how you continue to grow stronger in faith, being fully persuaded.

And being not weak in faith, he did not consider his own body, already dead (since was about a hundred years old), and the deadness of Sarah's womb. He did not at the promise of God through unbelief; but was strengthened in faith, giving glory to God; and being fully convinced that, what He had promised He was able also to perform. (Romans 4:19-21)

Abraham's faith grew stronger by rehearsing the promise that God made to him. His faith increased to the point to where he was fully persuaded that God was faithful to His Word. Sometimes you have to rehearse the promise of God over and over in your heart. Abraham never wavered in believing God's promise. When you waver in your faith, remember the faithfulness of God and the ability of God to perform what He promised. The performance of the promise is not in your ability, but in Gods.

HOLD FAST YOUR CONFESSION
Wherefore, holy brethren, partakers of the heavenly calling consider the Apostle and High Priest of our profession Christ Jesus.
(Hebrews 3:1 KJV)

Jesus is our Apostle and High Priest. As our High Priest, He pleads our cause before the Father. He intercedes on our behalf. He is representing you before the Father. He is the High Priest of our profession. The word profession also is rendered confession. The word confession comes from a word *"homologia"*, which means, *"to say the same thing."* Usually when you hear the word confession you might only think of it in the context of confessing of sin. You are repenting of your sins to God. You are coming into agreement with what God's word says about about your sin. However, the word confession may also be used in positive sense. If His Word states that you are healed, then that ought to be your confession. You are now saying the same thing as what His Word says. The scripture does not say that He is the High Priest of His confession, but rather our confession. Jesus is the High Priest of our confession. He can only function as our priest when our confessions agree with His will. If His Word says you are blessed, then don't confess you are broke. If we are saying something contrary to what His word reveals, then He cannot function as our High Priest. Make sure your confession agrees with the revealed will of God. While you are waiting for the manifestation of your prayer you must continue to hold firmly to your declaration of faith, because the one who made it is faithful.

Let us hold fast the confession of our faith without wavering; for He is faithful that promised. (Hebrews 10:23 KJV)

Hold firmly to your confession. Don't waver, don't bend even though the circumstances may look contrary. Do not let the enemy deceive you and cause you to change your confession. Before Abraham received his promise, God changed his name from Abram to Abraham. Every time he would introduce himself as Abraham he was confessing, or saying the same thing that God said, even before the promise manifested. Don't let the enemy change your confession and rob you of your manifestation.

RELEASING ANGELIC ASSIGNMENTS

One of the reasons why it is important for you to release your confession is because every time that you are speaking what you are believing for, you are giving angels their next assignments. Contrary to popular belief, angels are not little cute things that dangle from your rearview mirror.

When Daniel had understood that it was time for Israel to be released from captivity, he immediately went into prayer. He offered up the prayer of supplication. As soon as he prayed, God got involved and released an angel to give Daniel his request. However, while Daniel was praying, The Prince of Persia resisted the angel for 21 days, holding up Daniels answer, until Michael, one of the chief angels, came to assist the angel and bring Daniel his answer.

Now while I was speaking, praying, and confessing my sin and the sin of my people Israel, and presenting my supplication before the LORD my God for the holy mountain of my God: yes, while I was speaking in prayer, the man Gabriel, whom I had seen in the vision at the beginning, being caused to fly swiftly, reached me about the time of the evening offering. And he informed me, and talked with me, and said "O Daniel, I have now come forth to give you skill to understand. At the beginning of your supplication the command went out, and I have come to tell you, for you are greatly beloved (Daniel 9: 20-23)

If Daniel had not prayed, God couldn't release the

angel. I wonder how many angels are sitting on the sidelines waiting for us to pray. We have angels that are prepared to assist us. God's angels are powerful. They are warriors. They are mighty. They excel in strength. They are created by God to do His will. In other words, their assignment is to accomplish, execute, and advance the purpose of God. They have the charge of going about and gathering, governing and granting your answers. They are completely occupied to being industrious to procure the performance of God's Word. David says;

Bless the Lord, you His angels, Who excel in strength, who do His word, Heeding the voice of His word. (Psalm 103:20)

Angels are spirit beings created by God. Angels excel in strength. They have abilities to supersede any human strength. Angels have the ability to function in the realm of the spirit as well as the natural. Angels have assignments. Their objective is when they hear someone in the earth, a voice, that releases the Word of God, when they hear that Word there is a command from heaven that is given that they become the active agents in the earth to assist you. Angels are only activated when there is a voice that releases the word. The word *"heeding"* means *"to obey."* When angels hear a voice spoken by a believer, regardless of male or female, young or old, they obey the spoken Word of God. They help advance you. They are appointed to accomplish what you have been confessing. They go about gathering outcomes that are intended to advance your life in the earth for the cause of Christ. Angels are assigned to assist us in our prayer of supplication by executing the word of God that we profess.

You cannot just tell an angel do this or go there, but their directions are given from the Commander in Chief, when we speak the Word. They go about *"to do his commandments."*

When Daniel began to pray, his prayer had issued a license for heaven to get involved. I wonder what God wants to release in our lives today, but is unable to do so because we have tied his hands with our lack of prayer.

In the realm of the spirit, there is no time and there is no distance. Since there is no distance, then the moment that Daniel started speaking, an angel was released. Gabriel says, that at the beginning of the supplication, the very beginning when Daniel began to make claim on something due, God gave the command to the angel. God issued a decree. He gave an executive order from His throne, which sent the angel Gabriel his errand.

Then he said to me, "Do not fear, Daniel, for from the first day that you set your heart to understand, and to humble yourself before your God, your words were heard; and I have come because of your words.

(Daniel 10: 12)

In the amplified bible it states, **"I have come as a consequence and in response to your words."** God did not give the command until someone on earth who had begun to go into prayer and intercession. Once God heard someone in the earthly arena, God gave the order. Gabriel shows up as a response to Daniel's words.

Daniel had prayed for 21 days. Yet, the command was given the first day. The reason that it took the angel that long is because there was demonic interference in the second heaven trying to intercept the information the angel was bringing. Satan doesn't want you to get your breakthrough. He doesn't want you to get revelation that you are healed and you are blessed. He does everything that he can to intercept your miracle, your breakthrough, your answer to your prayers. He sets up demonic networks that cause disturbance in the heavens. Yet, Daniel kept on praying! He never fainted. He did not get weary. Do not allow delays distract you from pressing into God's promises for your life. Be confident in your seeking and knocking, knowing that you have received it and you are in alignment with God's purpose and will. It may very well be that there is warfare going on the heavens trying to block your answers from coming into your life.

Daniel's' words were the catalyst that activated angelic assistance. Daniel's prayer of supplication was instrumental in bringing about the purposes of God for the nation of Israel. God is searching for someone on the earth that will become His voice.

Praying God's words is the initiation of a shifting event that is evidence of faith on the earth that causes God to respond. God has promised to respond to His word, and God always keeps His promises.

While we are waiting for the manifestation of God's words to bear fruit, we are declaring, agreeing with, and confessing that promise. God is not just sitting back passively. He is engaged in watching over that word to perform it. Jeremiah 1:12 tells us; "You have seen well, for I am ready to perform My word."

God has promised that he will watch over His words to ensure that they manifest. It doesn't just mean that God is watching in hopes that it will happen. When He watches over something, His providential eyes begin to arrange events, connect people, and set up means and methods that are coordinating to your expected end. In the performance of God's words, there will oftentimes be other people that are designated to be a part of your answer. If in healing, God can bring it about supernaturally, or He may choose to utilize a specific doctor. In finance, He may use one bank that says yes when others said no. God will bring about the performance of His words. Therefore, it is crucial that your prayers be bathed in God's word.

9

Learning to Trust

*The preparations of the heart belong to man, But the
answer of the tongue, is from the LORD.
- Proverbs 16:1*

God wants to bring you the victory and release to
you the answers to your prayers even more than you
know. He has given us the of tool of prayer to do so.
It would be incomplete and misleading to say that
you are always going to get what you want.
Invariably, there will always seem to be times when
God seems to say "no" to our petitions. Sometimes
no means that it's not time, or not best for you. We
need to trust God for His timing as well as what is
best.

Learning to stand during these times of
uncertainty or disappointment is the greatest
challenge of a child of God. My father was a preacher
of the gospel and pastor of a church in Broken
Arrow, Oklahoma. He began his pastorate at the age
of 19. At the age of 58, he died from leukemia. My
father was a true pastor. He didn't like going out and

holding revivals. He wasn't looking for engagements from other churches. He just loved ministering and serving the flock that God had given him. The church sat on a large property, and even though they could hire someone to mow the lawn or even delegate it out, he did it himself. Not only did he cut the lawn himself, but it took 4 hours to mow the lawn on a riding mower. The amazing thing is that he continued to do while he was doing chemotherapy. He would do hours of chemotherapy and would be sick to his stomach and weak in his body but he continued doing what he was called to do. He continued to preach and sing even though he wore his "do rag" as he called it. He had a bandana to cover his head during the time of chemotherapy. He continued to preach the word, and sing songs of Zion; he loved to sing, and to continue to care for the flock of God. He was in the apex of his ministry; the church was growing. Then suddenly he transitioned from this life to the next.

Did we pray for his healing? Absolutely. Did we confess the word of God? All the time. Yet, even though we did everything we were supposed to do, he still passed away. I was devastated, hurt, disappointed. What happened to all my faith filled words? Why didn't it work? I prayed the Word, I confessed the Word over Him. I did all those things that I knew to do. Nevertheless, the outcome is not what I wanted. When things don't go the way that you hope or intend them to and you do everything that you know that you are to do, the question becomes *"Do you still trust Him?"* It is easy to trust God when you get your answers, but when things don't turn out, this is where you will find out if you trust God.

Trust in the LORD with all your heart; and lean not on your own understanding; In all your ways acknowledge Him, and He shall direct your paths. (Prov. 3: 5-6)

You may not even fully understand it all, but isn't this is what trust is about anyway. Do you trust Him even though you may not understand the *why's* of your life? One thing that I know is that sometimes God does not give us His reasons for not doing something. I'm glad God said no to some things in my life. I think that there were some things that I wanted that I thought would have been good, but it wouldn't be best. There were some doors God would not let me walk through, not because He didn't want to bless me but because He was protecting me from something I didn't even see coming. I've learned to trust Him even though things don't work out the way I wanted.

The heart of prayer is to develop such deep connection with God and knowing God so intimately that you submerged in His love and compassion that you completely trust him with the outcome.

The preparations of the heart in man, and the answer of the tongue, is from the LORD.

(Proverbs 16:1)

Yes, we are to do everything that we are instructed to do in the Word of God. We are to do our part in prayer, petition, and confession. However, the final reply or the answer of the tongue comes from the Lord.

ABOUT THE AUTHOR

Daniel Pringle is truly one of America's contemporary prophetic voices. He is a highly sought out keynote speak and author. His ministry imparts a cutting edge prophetic revelation that shifts people into a new dimension. His accuracy and precision in the demonstration of the gifts of the Holy Spirit has transformed countless lives. Prophet Pringle travels extensively across the nation and he has a burning passion to see regions transformed through the manifestation of God's presence.

Made in the USA
Columbia, SC
30 September 2017